INTO
Wild India

BLACKBIRCH®
PRESS

THOMSON

GALE

San Diego • Detroit • New York • San Francisco • Cleveland • New Haven, Conn. • Waterville, Maine • London • Munich

THOMSON
GALE

For more information, contact
The Gale Group, Inc.
27500 Drake Rd.
Farmington Hills, MI 48331-3535
Or you can visit our Internet site at http://www.gale.com

LIBRARY OF CONGRESS CATALOGING-IN-PUBLICATION DATA

Into wild India / Elaine Pascoe, book editor.
    p. cm. — (The Jeff Corwin experience)
Based on an episode from a Discovery Channel program hosted by Jeff Corwin.
Summary: Television personality Jeff Corwin takes the reader on an expedition to India to learn about the diverse wildlife found there.
Includes bibliographical references and index.
  ISBN 1-56711-854-2 (hardback : alk. paper) — ISBN 1-4103-0171-0 (pbk. : alk. paper)
  1. Zoology—India—Juvenile literature. [1. Zoology—India. 2. India—Description and travel. 3. Corwin, Jeff.] I. Pascoe, Elaine. II. Corwin, Jeff. III. Series.

  QL309.I68 2004
  591.954—dc21
                                                 2003009279

Printed in China
10 9 8 7 6 5 4 3 2 1

E ver since I was a kid, I dreamed about traveling around the world, visiting exotic places, and seeing all kinds of incredible animals. And now, guess what? That's exactly what I get to do!

Yes, I am incredibly lucky. But, you don't have to have your own television show on Animal Planet to go off and explore the natural world around you. I mean, I travel to Madagascar and the Amazon and all kinds of really cool places—but I don't need to go that far to see amazing wildlife up close. In fact, I can find thousands of incredible critters right here, in my own backyard—or in my neighbor's yard (he does get kind of upset when he finds me crawling around in the bushes, though). The point is, no matter where you are, there's fantastic stuff to see in nature. All you have to do is look.

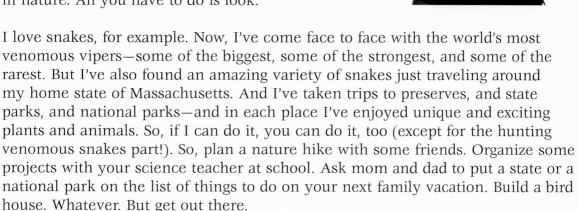

I love snakes, for example. Now, I've come face to face with the world's most venomous vipers—some of the biggest, some of the strongest, and some of the rarest. But I've also found an amazing variety of snakes just traveling around my home state of Massachusetts. And I've taken trips to preserves, and state parks, and national parks—and in each place I've enjoyed unique and exciting plants and animals. So, if I can do it, you can do it, too (except for the hunting venomous snakes part!). So, plan a nature hike with some friends. Organize some projects with your science teacher at school. Ask mom and dad to put a state or a national park on the list of things to do on your next family vacation. Build a bird house. Whatever. But get out there.

As you read through these pages and look at the photos, you'll probably see how jazzed I get when I come face to face with beautiful animals. That's good. I want you to feel that excitement. And I want you to remember that—even if you don't have your own TV show—you can still experience the awesome beauty of nature almost anywhere you go—any day of the week. I only hope that I can help bring that awesome power and beauty a little closer to you. Enjoy!

Best Wishes!

Jeff

Wildlife is everywhere in India. Over three hundred types of mammals and four hundred types of reptiles inhabit this land, and these creatures must coexist with 1 billion people, all in a country just half the size of the United States.

I'm Jeff Corwin.
Welcome to India.

India is a vast country.

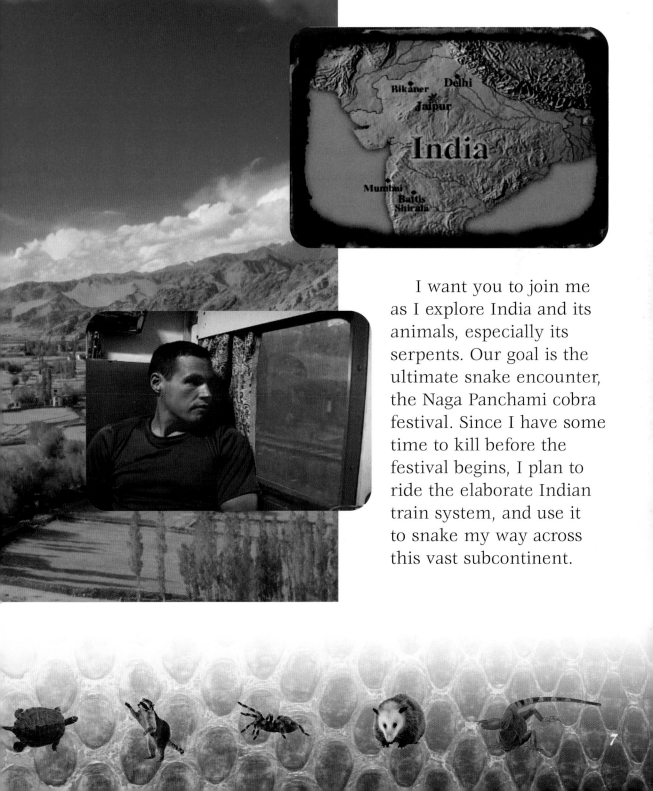

I want you to join me as I explore India and its animals, especially its serpents. Our goal is the ultimate snake encounter, the Naga Panchami cobra festival. Since I have some time to kill before the festival begins, I plan to ride the elaborate Indian train system, and use it to snake my way across this vast subcontinent.

We have just arrived in the village of Anjuna. It's a community deep in the interior of India, and what's great about this place is that its people, the Irula people, are masters at working with snakes.

This is Anjuna.

Years ago, the Irula would capture and kill snakes, and use the snakeskin or sell it to the leather industry. In the 1970s the Indian government made it illegal to capture and kill snakes, and the Irula community fell apart. But now they have a new plan. The Irula capture snakes and bring them back to a cooperative, where the snakes are milked of their venom. That venom is then turned into antivenin, the antidote to help people who are bitten, and the snakes are released back into the environment.

For an *amphibiophobiac*—that's someone who has an unnatural fear of snakes, this place could be the ultimate nightmare. But it's great for me because I get to go out with people that really understand the world of snakes.

The Irula people are snake experts.

Here's a snake ready to be milked.

Mutan, an Irula snake hunter, demonstrates how he catches cobras. He takes a stick and probes around, feeling for any movement. And we hit the lottery— we have a spectacle cobra, a very venomous snake, and very angry.

It's the first time I've actually captured a wild spectacle cobra, and now he's off to join some of his buddies at the Irula cooperative.

At the cooperative, the snakes are kept in earthen jars until they get their turn for venom extraction.

Each jar has a venomous cobra in it.

To collect the venom, the cobra has to be secured very carefully. Then we let him bite and eject venom naturally, just do it on his own, because we don't want to harm the snake. This venom will be dehydrated into a crystal and used to make antivenin. It's needed here— each year in India, venomous snakes bite over ten thousand people.

Milking a cobra.

This is a Russell's viper.

I'm like a kid in a candy store at the Irula cooperative. For my next piece of Jeff Corwin candy, I've picked a Russell's viper, a snake that is extremely, extremely aggressive. Not a nice snake, and it nearly gets away from me, but we extract some venom. We don't get much—this type of snake doesn't produce as much venom as some others. But the nature of this snake is extremely cantankerous. It's not a snake that you would ever want to mess with in the field.

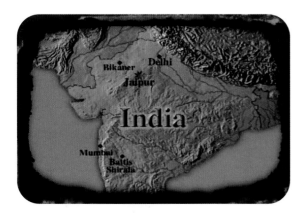

Temples everywhere...

Next up, Jaipur. Can you feel the energy in the air? It's electric. The air smells of exotic spices like cinnamon, cumin, curry…and elephant breath. The streets are filled with bustling markets, the screaming horns of buses and tractors…and elephants. The landscape is dotted with temples…and elephants.

...and elephants everywhere.

Animals in India are as common as taxicabs in New York City, adding an unpredictable and often deadly obstacle to an already difficult existence. Over the centuries, however, man and animal have formed a beneficial relationship, learning to work together. Probably the hardest-working and most relied upon animal in India is the mighty elephant.

It is time for the morning bath for these elephants. The gentlemen who are caring for them are called mahouts, and the relationship between elephant and mahout is extremely tight. When the elephant is a calf and the mahout is a young boy, that's when the relationship begins. It's a practice that has been going on in India for thousands of years.

Elephants love baths!

The bath is a very important part of the day for this elephant and the mahout. Elephants love to take baths. That's why these creatures are attached to ropes—when they're done and it's time to go to work, these animals aren't eager to leave. They like just to hang around in the water.

You do acquire a sense of authority riding an elephant, but for city traffic, they're not very practical. Let's hit the road by Jeep and do a little exploring.

Elephants are a major transportation source in India.

Another find...

...the desert sand boa.

Here's a creature that was definitely on my wish list to find here in India. This is the desert sand boa, or red sand boa. I don't need my stick or bag for this snake because it isn't venomous and it's not known for biting. When the desert sand boa feels threatened, he presses his head deep into the coil of his body. The head is the most sensitive part of this animal, and he wants to protect it. What he exposes is the end of his tail. At first glance you might think the tail was damaged, but this is the way it looks naturally. It actually looks just like this creature's head.

Heads or tails?

This is a really fun snake to watch because of the way it moves. Snakes usually slither along in a serpentine, or S-shaped, fashion.

These guys can move in a straight line.

But this snake has the ability to travel in a straight line, with what's called concertina movement. Much of its life is spent underground, in narrow tunnels, where it moves by wedging its coils against the sides of the tunnel and then extending its body straight ahead.

The Monkey Temple.

Hundreds of monkeys call this place home.

This complex of temples is commonly known as the Monkey Temple, due to the hundreds of monkeys that call it home. It was built at a natural spring, which flows down a mountain and fills a number of pools. The water in these pools is considered holy, and to bathe in them is a very sacred experience.

On the oxcart express!

I've hitched a ride on an oxcart, and just look at the way they've adorned the horns of the animals. Oxen and cows are considered sacred animals in the Hindu religion, and it's considered taboo to kill a cow for food. Cows provide milk and fuel, in the form of their waste. Cows and oxen are also an important source of labor. For example, you can use them to pull a plow, or in this case, pull a cart. India, a land of a thousand relationships between man and animal.

Our next destination is a temple that almost defies description.

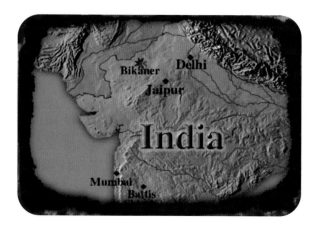

No shoes allowed.

We're in a small village called Deshnoke, outside Bikaner, in the middle of the Indian desert. Out of respect to the goddess Karni Mata, we've removed our socks and shoes to enter a very special place.

This is the Karni Mata icon.

The Temple of Karni Mata was established for a very important reason. Legend has it that a terrible sickness took the lives of many young children, and the parents pleaded with the goddess to revive their sons and daughters. Karni Mata is said to have obliged and brought each of the children back in the body of a rat.

In the temple you can see the icon of Karni Mata, and all around you'll see rats. And the rats are not pests here. In fact, this temple is dedicated to these rats. It's believed that when followers of Karni Mata die, they temporarily inhabit the body of a rat before being reborn as a human being.

Here, the rat is king.

Rats everywhere!

Rats here dine on milk mixed with honey and spices.

The white rat is the holiest.

From a silver bowl, the rats drink a sort of Hindu holy milk-shake—milk mixed with honey, sugar, and spices. After the rats are done, it's not uncommon for a believer to take this bowl and have a sip, and have the good luck from the rats pass on to the human being.

Luck is with us on our visit. Most of the rats are gray, but we see a white rat—considered the holiest of rats. A glimpse of the white rat is the highest blessing you can receive in this temple. I'm going to take advantage of the good fortune bestowed upon me by that white rat and see what other creatures we can find.

I'm going to try...

...to get on one of these...

Here's a nice herd of dromedaries, the type of camel that has one hump. Although I've always pictured India as a lush, tropical place, a lot of it is desert—and camels are perfectly designed to live in this challenging habitat.

and ride...

Even though these creatures are domesticated, there's nothing more cantankerous than a camel. They can bite, they can kick, and they can spit. I'll get the camel herder to negotiate with his animals, and get a ride.

I'm acting like a tree.

Aren't vine snakes gorgeous?

Look at this snake—is this not absolutely beautiful? This is a green vine snake. As long as I just let my limbs relax, he moves about me as if I were one of the trees where this creature lives. But as soon as I stop acting like a tree, he takes a defensive position. I have to be careful because he's venomous. He has rear fangs, and his venom is just strong enough to kill a lizard, a very small bird, or frog. Still, you never know how you're going to

Look at that head, and those eyes...

react to venom until you're bitten, and I don't want to take that chance.

Check out those eyes. He's got elliptical pupils, bright black. Have you ever seen a snake that is more elegantly designed, that is as beautiful as this green vine snake? That's about the brightest green you'll ever see in nature.

We're still on our way to the cobra festival, but some larger reptiles are waiting for us first, including one that thinks I might make a tasty snack.

Near Chennai, on India's eastern coast, is Crocodile Bank. It's one of only a few places in India that breeds and raises an endangered crocodile species called the gharial. Because they're having trouble finding natural habitat in which to release the animals, this facility is vital to the survival of these fascinating reptiles. Herpetologist Nick Whitaker, the manager here, shows us around.

The Indian gharial is one of the rarest types of crocodilians in the world, and I've

My friend Nick will show us around.

That's one unique-looking snout.

never had a chance to see one in the wild before. The name "gharial" comes from the term *ghara*, which means "water vessel," probably from the potlike structure on the end of this animal's snout.

He's looking at me...

Gharial eggs

Baby gharials are only about 12 to 14 inches long when they hatch, but they can grow up to 20 feet in length. A gharial can be completely submerged, invisible to anything above the water, but have a perfect view of the landscape because his eyes stick up on top of his head, just like a periscope.

A beautiful youngster.

Not only do I get to see gharials here, I actually get to handle a youngster. But I keep looking over my shoulder as I do because there are adult females in this lagoon. They're extremely protective of their offspring. Even though they

have not had any contact with these youngsters in two years, handling the animals could push them into monster mother role. Then before I know it, I'll have a gharial hanging off my leg.

See the gharial spying on me?

The population of these animals is higher in captivity than it is in the wild because so little of their natural habitat is left. We've figured out how to breed them in captivity. The next challenge is to figure out how to salvage habitat, so there's a place to reintroduce them.

In addition to the fabled gharial, this place is home to thousands of very irritable crocodiles. You can't see them all because the water is murky, but Nick says there are about 750 in this pool. Are you ready? We're going to capture

How about a dip in the pool?

Now hold still...

a female crocodile. In order to prevent the croc population from increasing any further, we're going to move her to a separate pond where she'll be unable to breed.

We move in, grab number 452, and pull her out. I sit on her neck and secure her mouth as Nick checks her over. All the strength in this creature's jaw is in the crunching, not in the opening— so as long as I secure her mouth, we should be okay.

I'm holding her down.

She's ready to go, and we need to move quickly—there are other crocs here that could jump out at us. As soon as we have her at the new pond, we release her jaws and let her go.

Now let's check out some snakes.

LOOK AT THIS!

There are nearly twenty-five different species of crocodilians in the world—divided into three main families. In the family *Gavialidae*, there's only one member: the gharial (or gavial).

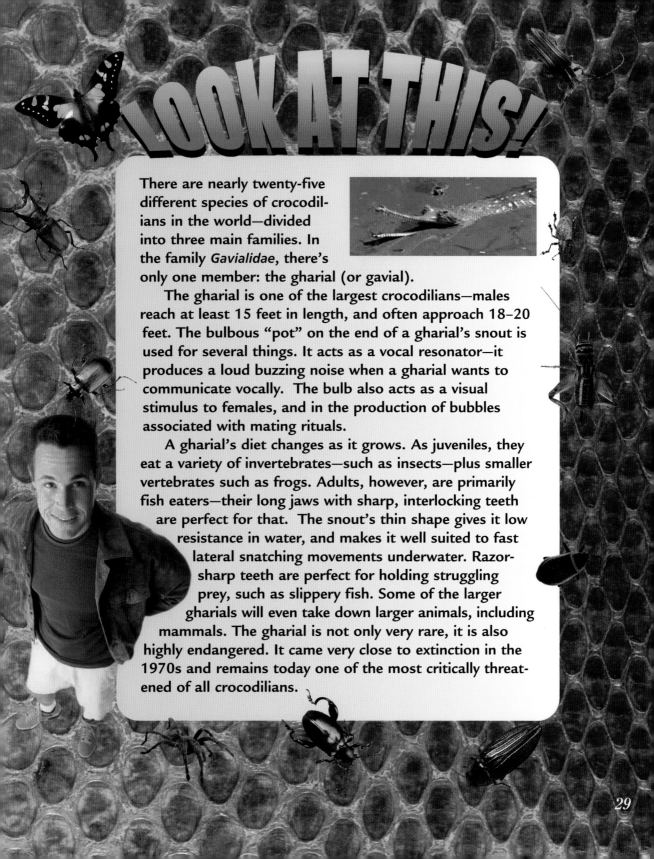

The gharial is one of the largest crocodilians—males reach at least 15 feet in length, and often approach 18–20 feet. The bulbous "pot" on the end of a gharial's snout is used for several things. It acts as a vocal resonator—it produces a loud buzzing noise when a gharial wants to communicate vocally. The bulb also acts as a visual stimulus to females, and in the production of bubbles associated with mating rituals.

A gharial's diet changes as it grows. As juveniles, they eat a variety of invertebrates—such as insects—plus smaller vertebrates such as frogs. Adults, however, are primarily fish eaters—their long jaws with sharp, interlocking teeth are perfect for that. The snout's thin shape gives it low resistance in water, and makes it well suited to fast lateral snatching movements underwater. Razor-sharp teeth are perfect for holding struggling prey, such as slippery fish. Some of the larger gharials will even take down larger animals, including mammals. The gharial is not only very rare, it is also highly endangered. It came very close to extinction in the 1970s and remains today one of the most critically threatened of all crocodilians.

In this tree is an animal that at one time was very common throughout India, but today is becoming increasingly rare due to habitat loss and overhunting. It's the Indian rock python, a totally beautiful creature.

It's a challenge to get the snake out if its tree, and she's not too happy about it. Once I have her, she wraps herself around my arm as if she's checking my blood pressure. Actually, this is how she protects herself. If she were to be

attacked by a preda-
tor, she would first
bite and then wrap
around her attacker.

She's wrapped really tight around my arm.

Most importantly,
though, this hug is
the way she kills her
prey. My arm is turn-
ing purple because
she's literally cutting
off the blood flow
from my body. If my
arm were a baby jackal or
some other small animal, it
would be literally squeezed
to death. Every time the
animal exhaled, the snake
would squeeze tighter.

There she goes...

We're going to put her
at the base of this tree
and let her go where she
wants to go.

I have to be very careful...

I'm holding a snake known as the common krait. If it's provoked and bites, that bite is deadly, absolutely deadly. You can die within a couple of hours of being bitten.

Look at the shape of this snake's muzzle and the way the eyes are set back along its rostrum, where the nostrils are. These features are typical of the group of snakes we call elapids.

See the way the eyes are set back?

If this snake is left alone, it will probably never mess with you. But if it should crawl into your bunk and you roll on it, or if you should step on it while you're working in the field, that's when you have problems.

You don't mess with these guys.

We finally arrived at the small town of Battis Shirala, which comes to life each year for the Naga Panchami festival. Agriculture is extremely important to the economy of this village, and the farmers spend a lot of time in the fields. They grow peanuts, corn, and squash, and where you have peanuts, corn, and squash you get rats. And those rats eat the crops and burrow into the earth. What goes after the rats? Snakes—including cobras.

More oxen riding...

Let's see what we find in the peanut field...

In this field of peanuts, we have a wonderful serpent. He's not a venomous snake, and I'm not worried about him biting me. This is a rat snake, a very valuable animal for the farmers here. They have great respect for snakes because these animals perform a very important function. Keep in mind that a quarter of the yield that comes from the peanuts or other crops would be lost to vermin like rats and mice if there were no snakes to prey on those creatures and keep their

Rat snakes like this are a big help to farmers.

What else can we find?

numbers down. That's why the farmers like snakes. And because he helps the farmers, we'll let this guy go do his work.

The farmers say they've found something else for us to see. Come on.

Wow! Look at this. I've got a cobra. One wrong move, and I'm in serious trouble. Isn't this beautiful?

Actually, there are cobras throughout these fields. Surrounded by these deadly snakes,

the farmers recognize the great dangers facing them each day. They overcome their fear of snakes and show their gratitude to the serpents by worshiping the cobra in an elaborate celebration. And that's what this festival is about, paying tribute to this beautiful snake. This tiny village of Battis Shirala, population seventeen thousand, will be flooded by over one hundred thousand visitors by the time the festival begins.

In preparation for the festival,

Here's a cobra among the peanut plants.

This festival celebrates the cobra.

Snake entrants get ready...

sixty-five groups have been collecting snakes for the past two weeks, and now it's all come to this final moment. There will be two winners—the team that has the fattest or heaviest snake, and the team that has the longest snake.

Measuring for the longest...

Weighing for the heaviest.

Handlers are experts.

An extended hood means the snake is angry.

A cobra can strike out horizontally only about the same distance it can raise itself vertically. That's how these handlers know they are far enough away to be out of range of the deadly bite. A handler has a safety zone of about three feet away from his snake. The handlers also know that the cobra will strike only when his hood is extended. These men do not fear the snakes. They believe a mutual respect between human and serpent exists. This festival, in honor of the reptile, ensures this everlasting bond.

One happy winner.

Some trophies are huge.

At the end of the contest, trophies are presented. The winners are covered in vermilion powder, and the celebration continues as everyone gears up for the festival climax. But the festival of Naga Panchami happens not only in the streets but also in the households. In fact, it's in the house that the most important ritual takes place.

Cobras are holy creatures in the Hindu religion. The cobra is known as Nag and is associated with Shiva, the god of destruction. So not only is the cobra a physically dangerous creature, it is a spiritually powerful being as well.

These snakes are an important part of a Hindu's spiritual life.

This is why, during the festival, cobras that have been captured by expert snake handlers are taken into homes and treated as honored guests. In this home, the woman of the house presents a tribute to Nag, offering milk to the snake. The man of the house sprinkles vermilion powder and puts a garland over the animal's head.

In the house, these cobras are treated as honored guests.

Offerings are made...

...and adornments are given.

I love experiences like this. Not only do we have a chance to travel to an exotic place and learn about the wildlife there, but we also get a little window into the culture that helps to make that land very rich. And here in India, we're learning about snakes, but we also have a chance to experience the relationship between people and snakes.

When the celebration is finished in the house...

Now that each family has conducted its own tribute to the cobra, the celebration is taken into the streets. Snakes are transported in clay pots and on floats, and some are even hand carried through the village in a

...it's taken to the streets.

Expert handlers are a major part of the festival.

Everyone wants a chance to worship the cobras...

...and to hold them.

procession accompanied by loud, festive music and cheers. It's the official start of the Naga Panchami festival—or, if a snake handler isn't careful, the official end.

Throughout the day snakes are continually worshiped, serving to further the harmonious relationship between the farming community and these deadly reptiles. The Naga Panchami festival is extremely important to the people here, but it's controversial. There is some measurable stress on the snakes, and for

This is my kind of festival!

that reason a lot of animal rights groups have problems with this holiday festival. I think that in an ideal world, it would be best to leave the cobras in the wild. But if you're going to have a relationship where human being and cobra come together, probably it's better that the snakes are worshiped rather than killed out of fear.

Our trip to India was wonderful! We saw snakes. We saw animals of all kinds. It was exhausting—but a great experience. I'll see you on our next adventure!

Glossary

antidote a remedy for a poison

antivenin the antidote for a snake's venom

crocodilian a type of reptile, such as a crocodile or alligator

dehydrate to lose water

dromedary a breed of camel

elapid a type of venomous snake

habitat a place where animals and plants live naturally together

herpetologist a scientist who studies reptiles

hindu the dominant religion in India

invertebrates species of animals without spinal columns, such as insects

mahout in India, a man who takes care of elephants

mammals warm-blooded animals that feed their babies with milk

reptile a cold-blooded, usually egg-laying animal such as a snake or lizard

serpentine resembling a serpent or snake

venom a poison used by snakes to attack their prey or defend themselves

vermilion a bright red pigment

vertebrate species of animals with spinal columns, such as dogs

viper a type of venemous snake

Index